THE

PRISONER OF CHILLON

BY

LORD BYRON.

WITH A SHORT DESCRIPTION OF THE CASTLE, AND A NOTICE

OF

THE CHIEF HISTORICAL EVENTS, AND LEGENDS CONNECTED WITH ITS HISTORY.

Selected from authentic sources by an English resident.

VEVEY.

Gabriel Blanchoud Editor,

PRINTED BY CH.-F. RECORDON AT VEVEY.

INTRODUCTION.

In a country where nature has clothed the landscape with outlines of harmonious beauty, and where history renders many objects interesting to the reflective mind, the traveller is attracted towards the scenery of the upper end of the Lake of Geneva by an admiration both of the visible and of the intellectual creation.

As the humble dewdrop reflects on its crystal surface the sky, earth, and surrounding scenes of a wide horizon, so the private history of a secluded site of the Alps casts a light on the past events of several ages. The small castle of Chillon has been favored, in a higher degree than would be supposed from its modest appearance, by the privilege of illustrating many of the remarkable æras of European history. The gigantic shadow of the middle ages, the pride of chivalry and feudal power, the light of Reform, and, above all, the inspirations of Byron, have crowned its simple but time worn walls with a halo of interesting reminiscences.

In offering to the public a short sketch of its real history and recollections, derived from the best local authorities, the author hopes to render a visit to the castle even more attractive, than when it has been merely viewed as having furnished the groundwork of an immortal poem.

DESCRIPTION.

The origin of the Castle of Chillon is buried in the darkness of the middle ages. Above one thousand years ago, there existed, on the site occupied by the present edifice, a massive tower, washed on all sides by the waters of the lake, which then rose many feet higher that at present, and connected by no drawbridge with the shore. This tower, to use the sense of an ancient chronicler, « was of lofty and narrow form, built above caverns, and inaccessible to any, save an angel sent by divine command » : it was even then employed as a prison for political offenders. It possessed no name, or at least none has been handed down by history, unless it were the « *Caput laci* » mentioned in a monkish account of the translation of the relics of St. Marcellinus. Thence the captive could see nothing but the sky, the Pennine Alps, and the Lake Leman; the road, by which it was approached, wound along the foot of the rocks, where they descend from the outworks of the Naie to the shore of the Lake.

These details bear so great a resemblance to the characteristic features of the present edifice, that we may venture on believing the solitary tower to have existed on the same site.

The Castle of Chillon, *Zillium* and *Gillum* in 1218, *Castrum de Chilione* in 1236, is a strong building in the Gothic style, founded on a rock, which is by some authors supposed to have rolled down from the mountain above. It was formerly surrounded by the waters of the lake, and still communicates with the land by a drawbridge; the descent of the water level has left a dry ditch on its Nord East side, while, on the South and West, the lake at its base is full 700 feet in depth.

As the communication between Italy and West Switzerland was formerly limited to this narrow defile, it was a very important position, in days when the use of artillery was unknown, especially as two horsemen abreast could barely pass along the road, which wound between the mountain and its walls.

On the slope of the hill, which descends towards the castle there existed in ancient times a village called the « *Bourg de Chillong* »; this place was ruined by some means of which the details are unknown, and its inhabitants retired to the present hamlet of *Veytaux*.

A stone gateway on the west of the Castle, built to intercept the passage in feudal times, was demolished half a century ago for the enlargement of the road.

The first authentic mention of the present castle is contained in a donation made by Humbert 2nd, Count of Savoy and Marquis of Italy, who died in 1103, to the Abbey of *Haut Cret*, of certain lands near his castle of Chillon, with exemption from all manner of taxes, and free passage over his lands, expressly charging his Seneschal and officers at Chillon to see to the punctual execution of the same. This charter sufficiently proves its existence, both at and before that epoch.

In 1161, a Burgess of Vevey, Jacques de Cojonnay, gave to the same religious foundation a fief at Montreux, on condition that the Monks should bear their quota of the expenses of the guard of Chillon.

In 1248, Count Peter of Savoy, surnamed on account of his military talents « the little Charlemagne », having appreciated the importance of the position for ensuring his new conquests in the Canton de Vaud, considerably augmented the fortifications of Chillon, and may be considered as the founder of the present edifice.

The architecture of this ancient building in no way differs from that of other monuments of the feudal age. Its massive and irregular walls, flanked by six towers, and surmounted by turrets, with loop holes and battlements, bear every appearance of having been constructed at different periods.

The square tower in the centre is a very lofty keep, whence the eye commands almost the whole Lake and its borders; it still contains the alarm bell, which summoned the inhabitants of the country to the defence of the castle.

In the other towers are observed all the instruments of feudal tyranny — those deep and darksome dungeons where the captive lingered till hope had sickened into despair, and the memory of his existence had passed away from the minds of the living — the chamber of the question, where torture full often compelled from the innocent, to gain in death a respite from racking pains, the confession of crimes imagined by accusing tyranny.

The habitable parts of the castle are composed of two stories above the vaults. In the upper suite the Duke of Savoy often resided with his family. One of the principal rooms, called « the hall of knights », is supported by three columns; it separated the servants' lodging from the Duke's chamber, which communicated by a side door with that of the Duchess. The latter room commands an extensive view of the Lake and mountains : that of the Duke looks out upon the inner court of the castle, and receives the light from a window adorned with allegorical figures. John of Grandson, an artist of 1342, embellished its walls with subjects taken from the hunting scenes of the middle ages, and represented on the ceiling and rafters a profusion of fleurs de lys with the white cross of Savoy.

From the prince's apartment, some steps descend to an ancient chapel, formerly embellished with rich frescoes, of which modern whitewash has left no trace. The service of the established protestant church of Switzerland takes place here every Sunday.

The lower suite of apartments was employed in the time of the Dukes of Savoy as a residence for the seneschal. The kitchen and the vast dining hall, supported by columns of carved oak, contain abundant space for the exercise of feudal hospitality. The justice hall communicates with the dungeons by a staircase, and the other vaulted chambers appear to have been used as arsenals or store rooms for the garrison.

The dungeons of Chillon, hewn in the foundation rock, extend for a space of near a hundred yards in length beneath the castle; they do not lie below the waters of the lake, as has been often said and sung, for its highest level is near nine feet lower. They are divided into several cells of various sizes; the two largest are beneath the dining and justice halls, and between them are two dark recesses, destined for the execution of criminals, from one of which the staircase leads up to the justice halls. A beam black with age is shewn here, to which the victims were suspended, and a basin wherein many thousand Jews are said to have been decapitated in the 13th century, when a kind of plague, called «*the black death*», caused great ravages, and their nation was accused of a widely spread conspiracy for poisoning all the public fountains in Europe. The vault of the last and most extensive dungeon is supported by seven columns, inscribed with numberless names of the most eminent personages of the century. It receives a feeble daylight through long narrow openings in the wall, from one of which Byron supposes the « *lovely bird with azure wings* » to have carolled to the captive.

These underground apartments are by some persons imagined to have been, in the first instance, intended as a place of refuge for the female and infant population of the environs, in times of the approach of an enemy, when the alarm bell summoned the male population to man the walls. Full many prisoners, whose sufferings have gained no sympathy, because no bard has sung their woes, have here ended their days by violent death or by slow lingering decay. History in one instance, in another a poetic fiction engrafted on truth, have handed down to us the names of two captives; in the 9th century, *Wala*, the relative and friend of Charlemagne, and, in the 16th, *Bonivard*, one of the champions of the Reformation. An account of some passages of their history, and a few anecdotes of the most remarkable personages who have illustrated the castle, may perhaps be interesting.

The Count Wala. A. D. 830.

At the death of Charlemagne, when the elements of the vast empire he had founded by his mighty sword and governed with a sagacity far beyond his æra, seemed in imminent danger of dissolution, the eyes of all classes were turned towards a man, whom in the last years of his life the emperor had honored with his entire confidence — his cousin the Count Wala, a grandson of Charles Martel, who had governed Saxony and often commanded the Imperial armies — a man, says his historian Radbert, « true in speech, just in judgment, provident in council, faithful in trust . . . whom neither the terror of threats, nor the force of circumstances, nor hope of the present, nor dread of the future, neither promises of reward, nor endless kinds of punishment, could call away from the charity of Christ. »

First among all the great Lords of the Empire, he paid homage to Lewis the Debonair, on which the rest, with no farther hesitation, followed his example. Having been honoured above others by the friendship of Charlemagne, Wala was devoted to the continuation of his ideas, and to the preservation of the unity of the Empire, by an alliance of its Roman and Germanic elements. In later times an opposition of principles bred collision between him and Lewis, for Wala dreaded that the weakness of the monarch might cause the ruin of the state, and Lewis feared Wala, as a reflection of the mighty shade of his departed father.

The new king of the Franks was, like his father, a man of majestic stature and handsome features, but his monkish education tended to impress him with a servile respect for the church, and to crush the development of his manly qualities. He soon became the victim of court intrigues, and a weak instrument in the hand of designing counsellors. Yielding to their influence, he exiled the ancient friends of his father. Adelhard, the elder brother of Wala, was banished to the island of Noirmoutier at the Mouth of the Loire. Others were confined in monasteries, and Wala retired to that of Corbia in Picardy, an establishment which his family had founded.

His simple and conciliating manners soon gained the affection of the monks, and he was chosen Abbot of the monastery. In the direction of his new charge he displayed much activity, « like a father to all, bearing his sheep on his shoulders, neglecting nothing which might tend to the salvation of the souls confided to him. » During journeys he allowed no preparation to be mode for lodging on the way, no tent by day or night; but he and his attendants slept on the grass, or in the deep furrows of the fields.

This peaceful retreat was troubled by news of imprudent concessions of the Emperor Lewis to the church, which had alienated the laity, and disposed them to insurrection. Such conduct was unfavorably contrasted with that of his father Charlemagne, who had shewn in very precise language his opinion of priestly exaction. « Let me know in truth, said he, what you mean by saying you have quitted the world. Tell me, if he has quitted the world, who, every day, by every means, by every sort of artifice, tends unceasingly to augment his possessions, — who with this view, one day by menacing with the pains of hell, another day by promising heavenly rewards, seeks to persuade the simple, rich and poor alike, to despoil themselves and their lawful heirs of the goods which belong to them? Tell us, if he has quitted this world, who, desirous of another man's goods, buys perjured witnesses, and adresses himself to a dishonest judge to acquire what does not belong to him? Tell me lastly, what to think of those, who, under pretext of the love of God, his saints and martyrs, transport from place to place the relics of saints to get new churches built, and induce men by all sorts of arguments to give or bequeath their property to these churches? »

They soon learnt at Corbia, that Lewis, in accordance with the wishes of the people, had divided the Empire among his three sons. His nephew, Bernard, whose rights had been overlooked, had recourse to arms, but was induced to come to the Imperial court, where he was cast into prison and mur-

dered, after having had his eyes put out. This cruel act was
committed without the privity of the Emperor, who was
struck with horror on learning it, and subjected himself to the
severest penance for a crime which was not his own. He
recalled Wala, with other old friends of his father, to the
court, and begged him to accompany his son Lothaire into
Italy. The Abbot of Corbia complied with this request, bent
on the consolidation of the Empire, which seemed near the
verge of its ruin.

In Italy he did much for the reestablishment of good order;
his biographer relates an anecdote characteristic of the times.
A noble widow, despoiled of her fortune by a corrupt admi-
nistrator, laid a complaint before the Emperor. The judges,
to whom the matter was referred, proved corrupt; where-
upon Wala took her under his own protection. He had sent
to assemble the witnesses, when he learnt that she had been
assassinated by the man who had injured her. Upon this the
offender by his means was dragged before the court, but the
crime was resolutely denied, and the judges, gained over by
bribes, were on the point of pronouncing an acquittal, when
Wala, by the power of his eloquence, wrung from the traitor
the avowal of his crime.

The enormous wealth and rapacity of the church had ex-
cited the jealousy of the temporal Lords, who often laid waste
the ecclesiastical domains, hoping, by open violence, to regain
what had been extorted from the devotion and superstitious
fears of their ancestors. The public suffered from this state of
confusion to such a degree, that Wala, with the rude frank-
ness of the times, laid his complaint before the Emperor.

These efforts were vain, for Lewis was completely led
astray by the perverse counsellors who surrounded him, and,
in the end, the Church, as well as the lay nobles, accused
Wala of a desire to stir up discord in the court, and treated
him as a public enemy. The only course left open for him
was to retire to Corbia, where, among the monks, like a
second Jeremiah, he wept over the evils of his country.

About this period the Emperor married Judith of Bavaria, a

beautiful but crafty princess, to whose son Charles, after-
wards named the Bald, he desired to grant an inheritance to
the prejudice of the three elder. Many serious accusations
were brought forward against Judith, and the three princes
took up arms against their father, who was abandoned by all,
and fell into their hands.

Uncertain what course to adopt after their success, the vic-
tors applied to Wala for advice. He recommended them to
restore their father to the throne, after banishing his faithless
wife, and evil counsellors. This recommendation was unfavo-
rably received, and when a sudden change of popular opinion
had restored the Emperor to the throne and humbled his sons,
Wala, whose sincere advice had been alike distasteful to all
parties, was committed prisoner to Chillon by order of the
Empress and her minister Bernard.

At that period the culture of the vine had not embellished
the banks of the Lake, wild plants grew from rock to rock,
and a solitary chapel existed on the site of the present
village of Montreux. The ravages of the Lombards, as well as
of the robber nobles of the neighbourhood, had caused the
population to prefer the pastoral life of the retired valleys of
the Alps; the recent fall into the lake of Mount Tauretunum,
when a monstrous wave had swept away so many towns and
villages, had prevented settlers from venturing to inhabit its
banks. The tower of Chillon was then looked on as a dismal
solitude and an abode of desolation.

Such was not the impression produced on the Abbot Wala
at the sight of its dark walls. He believed that the Eternal
word held constant communion with the faithful, and his trust
in God, an inexhaustible source of consolation, preserved him
from discouragement. There he remained several years, visi-
ted by no one, says his biographer, save the angels, which in
all places know how to arrive at the heart of the good man.

At length this same author, Pascasius Radbert, succeeded in
obtaining permission to visit his friend, charged with a conci-
liatory message from the Emperor. He relates, in a style of
touching simplicity, the details of their intimate conversations,

in which he sought to persuade Wala to make some advances towards his sovereign, but all arguments failed in presence of the unbending rectitude of one who was conscious of no wrong.

His captivity at Chillon continued, until the three sons of Lewis had again risen in insurrection against their father, when, on account of the insecurity of Chillon, he was conveyed through the midst of France to the island of Noirmoutier at the mouth of the Loire. No sooner had he arrived there, than the fear of his liberation by one of the Emperor's sons induced his enemies to transport him to the extremity of Germany, where he was received in the monastery of Fulda; but, as Lewis of Bavaria, the third son of the Emperor, was approaching that district, he was allowed to return to his Abbey of Corbia, on condition of living as a simple monk, and in submission to the rules of the convent.

Shortly after his arrival there he received the visit of deputies from the Pope, as well as from the Emperor's sons, all of whom earnestly solicited his return to public life, as the only man capable of guiding the helm of state. On his refusal to comply, they were about to drag him forcibly from his retreat, when he yielded at length to their urgent demand, and set out for the court accompanied by his faithful Radbert.

The journey was perilous, for, from all sides of the Empire, troops of armed men were advancing with hostile intentions towards the Rhine, some as partizans of the old Emperor, others to support the Princes his sons. Often these living streams crossed, and even came into collision with each other. On arriving, Wala presented himsef to the Emperor, and all the influential churchmen attached themselves to his person. Pope Gregory the 4th was striving to mediate between the contending parties, when the Gordian knot was untied in an unexpected manner.

The rival camps had approached each other; brothers in arms, who had served together under the standard of Charlemagne, had recalled the recollections of old times — the two armies were confounded in one — perhaps even the influence of gold was not foreign to the result ; but sure it is, that when Lewis awoke, as from a dream, he found himself a captive to his own sons. These events occurred about the end of June 836, nineteen years after the death of Charlemagne, near Colmar, on a meadow at the foot of Mount Siegwald, called the Red field (Rothfeld) or the Field of falsehood.

History relates the patience of Lewis under affliction, his persevering refusal to abdicate the Empire, and the total anarchy of the age, until the dissensions among his sons caused a renewal of the feeling of interest and respect for his person. It seemed as if mankind, blindfolded, were striking at random in the darkness, heedless of those on whom the blows fell.

One day, Wala surprised the chief officers of Lothaire in the act of arranging a division of the Empire among themselves. Confused at his presence, they asked his counsel, « All is very well, said he, save that you have left nothing to God of what belongs to him alone, and that you have taken no account of the wishes of honest men. »

Finding his advice was set at nought Wala resolved to leave all parties to their own course, and departed, in spite of the efforts of Lothaire, and Lewis, to detain him. This time he passed before the tower of Chillon, on his way to Italy, where he entered the convent of Bobbio in Lombardy, founded two centuries earlier by the zealous Irish missionary St. Columba.

He became Abbot of the Convent, and had reestablished the discipline of the founder within its walls, when, at the earnest prayer of Lothaire king of Italy, who desired to be reconciled to his father, and begged Wala to terminate his virtuous life by a good action, he again left his peaceful retreat for the scene of courtly intrigues.

This time he was received by the Emperor and Empress with the utmost deference and cordiality. All parties were weary of discord, and, as Wala held full powers to negotiate on the part of Lothaire, an arrangement was speedily effected.

Rejoicing in his success, he returned to the other side the Alps, where, being seized by an epidemic fever then reigning, he had barely time to arrive at Bobbio, and breathe his last

among his brethren. He died August 31ᵗ 836, anxious, rather
for the fate of his country, and of Lothaire, than for himself.
« Happy, says his biographer in conclusion, is the man who
suffers temptation, for, when he has been proved by the trial,
he shall receive the crown of life. »

During the three following centuries, history is silent on
the subject of the fortress of Chillon. It passed with the
neighbouring territories of Western Helvetia, from the Carlo-
vingian emperors to the kings of Burgundy, then to their
heirs the Emperors of Germany, and afterwards to the Counts
of Maurienne, who became Counts of Savoy.

The Bishop of Sion, about the period which followed the
decline of the empire, had taken advantage of the relaxation
of the sovereign authority, to extend his temporal rule over
the part of his diocese, which is now comprised in the Canton
de Vaud, and was limited by the *Oyonnaz*, a brook between
La Tour de Peilz and *Vevey*. The valley of the Rhone, Mon-
treux, and its environs, were subject either to the Church of
Sion, or to the rich monastery of St. Maurice. The Counts of
Savoy held Chillon, as a fief under the Church of Sion, which
also possessed Montreux.

Peter of Savoy or the little Charlemagne.

In the 13ᵗʰ century, the castle of Chillon began to acquire
its historical importance and present form.

Among the reigning families of Europe, none have displayed
greater political skill, or have turned to so good an account
the advantages of their position, as masters of the passes of the
Central Alps, than the ancestors of the present king of Sardi-
nia. First as Counts of the sterile province of Maurienne, then
as Counts or Dukes of Savoy, that illustrious house has, from
the middle ages to the present day, furnished a succession of
able statesmen and distinguished warriors.

At the commencement of the 13th century, the court of Thomas the 1st of Savoy was in high renown, as a school of chivalry. He left eight sons and two daughters, the younger of whom, Beatrice, became mother of the three queens of England, France, and Naples, and of an Empress of Germany.

Peter, one of the younger sons, with a view to the aggrandisement of his family, had entered the church, and, as Provost of the Cathedral of Lausanne, had governed the diocese from 1229 to 1231.

On the death of his father, he abandoned the ecclesiastical career, which political motives had compelled him to adopt, and in 1233 married Agnes, daughter of the Count of Faucigny. Jointly with Aymon, another of the eight brothers, he took up arms against their elder brother Amedeus, heir to the crown of Savoy; to prevent effusion of blood, the dispute was settled by a cession of the Chablais (which then included the valley of the Rhone, from the St. Bernard downward, as well as all the south side of the Lake, with the north bank to the Veveyse) to Aymon, and of some castles at Bugey and in the environs of Geneva to Peter. As Aymon was incapacitated from exertion by an incurable malady, all the power was concentrated in the hands of his brother. A confusion of interests and of territorial rights caused constant collisions between them and the Prince Bishop of the Valais, in the course of which Peter founded numerous castles to command the different passes.

Aymon, after residing some years at Chillon for the benefit of his health, and founding a chapel and hospital for poor, or necessitous pilgrims, at Villeneuve, died of leprosy in 1241.

The old chronicler says that Peter was « haughty, bold, and terrible as a lion, so brave that he was called the second Charlemagne, and knowing how to guide himself in such a manner as to subject many to his domination. »

After some success in a campaign against the Count of Genevois, he turned his views towards Lausanne, where, in 1249, he strove, by force of money and arms, to ensure the election of his brother Philip to the vacant Bishoprick. Another

faction seconded the claims of John of Cossonay. Both parties
had recourse to fire and sword; in the hottest of the tumult the
whole town was burnt down, but the combat was resumed
amid the smoking ruins. The surrounding country was in
arms. To support his brother, Peter had arrived at the head
of 6000 men. Most of the powerful barons of the neighbour-
hood the Counts of Gruyere, Estavayer, Cossonay, Fruence,
and others, with 1000 Bernese, had taken up the quarrel for
the opposite party; and, although hostilities continued some
time without any decisive result, Philip of Savoy in the end
abandoned Lausanne. During the struggle, Peter left for Eng-
land, invited by his niece Eleanor, queen of Henry IIIrd.

. This monarch, in the course of his long life, caused great dis-
contentment among his subjects by a preference for foreigners,
on whom he lavished his favours. Nevertheless the historians
of that day, Matthew Paris and others, whatever may have
been the irritation against such persons, make a favourable
exception with regard to Peter, who seems, by the simplicity
and nobleness of his manners, to have gained the general
esteem. He was created Earl of Richmond, but could not (as
the chronicle of Savoy erroneously asserts) have received the
order of the Garter, which did not yet exist, and his brother
Boniface was raised to the dignity of Archbishop of Canter-
bury.

« It happened one day », says the Chronicle of Savoy,
« while the Count Peter was at the court of his niece the
queen of England, who much loved to see him, and whilst he
was receiving the order of the Garter, and that numberless
jousts, tournaments, dances, banquets, devisings of new fa-
shions, and joyous inventions were going on, — it happened, I
say, that his governor of the Pays de Vaud, after having taken
counsel with the lords and chief men of the country, sent him
a secret message. They gave him to know, that the Count of
Genevois, day and night, thought only of taking from him his
dominion in Vaud, of exciting to rebellion the Lords of the
Country, promising he would give them such aid, that Peter
should neither hurt, nor oppress them; — finally, that men

2

posted by the Count in some places within the frontiers of Vaud, to wit in the castles of the Clées and Rue, caused all the griefs, damages, spoilzie and displeasure they could to the people of Savoy and Vaud.

Such speed did the messenger make, that he found the Count Peter, his Lord, in the chamber of the queen Eleanor, playing with the Ladies at a game called : *what are you carrying on your back?* And immediately when the Count Peter saw the courier of his Bailiff of Vaud, he retired to him, and asked for the letters he had, which the messenger kissed, and gave him, and on reading them the Count Peter reddened ; but without taking further notice, he returned to play with the ladies, who put a pillow of cloth of gold on his shoulders, and then asked him : « *What are you carrying on your back!* » — « *I carry Rue and les Clées in Vaud.* » — Then said the queen : « *Thou answerest not well, fair. uncle?* » — Then the ladies again asked him : « *What are you carrying on your back?* » — « *Rue and les Clées in Vaud.* » — « *You speak not to the purpose,* » said the ladies, and again asked him ; whereto he would not answer otherwise. Then the queen, who was a very prudent lady, knew that her uncle had received some news whereat he was greatly vexed. Soon she took him apart, and asked him : « What news have you, fair uncle, tell me, I pray you ; for methinks your are in anger? » — « My lady niece, said the Count, it is true that the Count of Genevois and I, being little children and playing together at chess, it fell out that I gave him a blow in the face, and he too hit me with the chess board on the head, and since then never were we friends, though we be cousins german. And, ever since, he hath sought to do me all the harm he can, so much that I, having, thanks to God, conquered and gained the country of Vaud, save two places, les Clées and Rue, he hath, since my departure, by the means of those two places, striven to make the people of the country rebel, and daily doth them all the harm he can ; which thing I hardly take in patience, and it is, as I told you, a heavy load on my back. Now I have considered, that if it pleased the king to deign aid me secretly by some of

his people, I should gain on my first arrival, and without
having to compose an army in my country, not only the said
fortresses, but all the country of Vaud. » — « Fair uncle, said
the Queen after having heard him, let me do as I please, and
I will see to it, for the king loves you, and moreover he will
do somewhat for me ; so be of good cheer. »

When the evening came, and the king and queen had reti-
red, the queen began to sigh. « What ails you? » said the
king, who loved her much. « It is true that the Count of
Geneva doth mighty wrong to my uncle of Savoy, and that
he hath news of it which vex him much, and I pray you, Sir,
to bestow on him aid, comfort, and counsel. » — « Let us sleep,
answered the king, and the night will furnish counsel. »

On day arriving, the king sent for Count Peter, and said to
him : « Why, fair uncle, do you set women to speak to me of
your affairs? We ought not to speak to women of important
matters ; for them I will do nought, but, for you, everything
possible. » Whereupon most humbly the Count Peter thanked
the king, and the king granted him men, archers, and
pioneers, as many as he would, and wherewith to arm 4000
men, with whom, when they were assembled, this Count
Peter took leave of the court, then quitted England, no one
knowing what he meant to do ; and made all haste they could,
by day and night, until they arrived before the castle of les
Clées in the country of Vaud. Having arrived there, he divided
his people into two parts, of whom he sent one to besiege Rue,
and placed the other at the siege of les Clées, in order to shew
his double power. And immediately he proclaimed throughout
all the country, to have succour and reinforce his army. And
so well did it fall out, that every one took up arms, with
good heart, so that Rue et les Clées were easily taken, and
their defenders yielded themselves up, on promise of life and
goods saved. Thence Peter of Savoy designed to go, and meet
his enemy the Count of Geneva. »

The report of the aid furnished by the king of England so
alarmed the Count of Geneva, that he consented to a peace,
whereby the castles in dispute were absolutely ceded to Peter,

who consented to pay a sum of money for their surplus value
beyond the expenses of the campaign.

Continuing his successes, he defeated the Valaisans, and
the lieutenant of the Emperor of Germany, in a well contested
battle at Portvalais, near the head of the Lake of Geneva ;
thence he pursued his flying enemies along the great Rhone
valley. At Martigny he effected a junction with his brother
the Count Amedeus, and both marched on Sion, which they
took after a tremendous assault. Castle after castle was stor-
med, and no breathing time allowed the enemy, until the
standard of Savoy was planted on the very snows of the Furka,
where the source of the Rhone is said to issue from the gates
of eternal night.

A precious trophy of these victories was the ring of
St. Maurice, commander of the massacred Theban legion,
which Peter compelled the Abbot and monks of the convent of
St. Maurice to yield up to him. He wore it till his death, and
the relic could not be alienated, or worn by any, but the
direct heir of the house of Savoy.

Sometimes, by peaceful purchase of disputed rights, more
frequently by victories, the Count Peter extended his dominion
on all sides of the Lake of Geneva, and well nigh founded an
absolute monarchy over all the Romand countries, where the
Gallo-Latin tongue was spoken. All the nobility of West
Switzerland, and even the barons of the valleys of the Ober-
land, bent the knee in homage to his power. Except Fribourg,
every town and castle, from the Léman to Berne, had opened
its gates and accepted his protection.

His chief strong hold was the castle of Chillon, which he
may be said to have constructed, and which formed his arse-
nal. Its approach was defended by a tower at the foot of Mont
Sonchaux, and, during his absences in England, the troops
were commanded by his faithful Hugh de Grammont. Napoleon
Bonaparte, the conqueror of Italy, incribed on the entrance of
the great Simplon road « ære Italo », and with equal justice,
might Peter of Savoy have engraved on the front of Chillon
« ære Anglico », inasmuch as the sums which paid for his

acquisitions, and the nerves of war which consolidated the work of subjection of his territories, were chiefly drawn from England.

There appeared great probability, that the house of Savoy was destined to reestablish the ancient Burgundian kingdom, since the prosperity of that dynasty was.farther increased, when, at the death of Boniface Count of Savoy, the sceptre of his house was conferred on Peter. He commenced his reign by taking Turin, and avenging the reverses of his predecessor on the other side the Alps. His power had now attained its apogee; the pope and the Emperor eagerly sought his friendship, and his influence maintained peace between the courts of France and England.

But a reverse was at hand; in the latter country, the weakness and prodigality of Henri IIIrd, as well as the favours showered on foreigners, among whom Peter of Savoy was the most eminent, in the end caused a general rebellion. All the domains, which had been granted him in England, were confiscated, and, in. fruitless efforts to come to the assistance of the Regal power, his own resources were well nigh exhausted. Amid these circumstances he returned to Switzerland, where his ancient enemies had once more raised the standard of revolt.

The chief of this coalition was Rodolph of Habsbourg, head of the house of Austria, who, in East Switzerland, was commencing a career, as glorious as that of Peter of Savoy in the west. After the death of Hartmann Count of Kibourg, in 1264, the favour of Richard of Cornwall, one of the claimants to the Imperial crown of Germany, and brother of Henry of England, had obtained for the Count of Savoy important fiefs held under the Empire.

Rodolph marched against the Pays de Vaud at the head of 1500 knights and a formidable infantry, while, on every side, the towns and nobility, who had borne the yoke of the house of Savoy, rose in formidable insurrection. Piedmont, Dauphiny, the Valais, Geneva, and the Pays de Vaud were drawn into a general league.

In spite of advancing years, and an exhausted treasury, the Count, with unexampled genius and activity, made head against his foes. During 1265, and the commencement of 1266, he gained some slight advantages, and at last, resolving on a decisive action, with the aid of 500 Bernese, he reduced the Valais after a war of stratagems, surprises, and pillage.

In the mean while, the chief confederate army had advanced to form the siege of Chillon. Germans, Vaudois, and the nobility of the environs were commanded by a lieutenant of Rodolph of Habsbourg, termed by ancient chroniclers the Duke of Coppinguen or Zoffinguen, who probably was no other than a younger Count of Kybourg.

They had commenced the siege, when the Count of Savoy, riding in silence, and concealing his approach under the shades of night, issued from the gorges of the Valais and approached the Lake.

« Without being perceived, says the history, the Count Peter made a sign to the warder of the castle, and having made himself known, he entered Chillon with two attendants. And when he was within, he refreshed himself, and drank; and those of the castle were mightily glad. Soon after, he mounted on the tower, from which place he could recognize and observe his enemies, and saw that they had their lodgings one far from the other, and were asleep, doubting of nothing. Then he descended, and got on a small boat, which soon bore him to Villeneuve, where he had left his people. And he came to them with much cheerfulness. When they saw him so joyous. « *What news?* » they asked him. « *Fair and good* », answered he, « *for with God's help, if we hold good, all our foes are in our hands.* » Whereto they all said with one voice : « *My Lord, you have but to command* ». And they armed themselves, and having made ready, mounted horse in good order, traversed the pass of Chillon without sound of trumpet, and suddenly fell on the tents and quarter of the Duke of Coppinguen, who offered small resistance, for they found him and his people disarmed, half awake, half asleep. And so well did they, that the Duke was taken prisoner. And with him were taken the Counts of Nidau, Gruyères, Arberg, and the Barons of Montfaucon, of Grandson, of Cossonay, of Montagny; in all eighty barons, lords, knights, squires and gentlemen of the country. And all of them did the Count Peter conduct into the castle of Chillon, where he treated them not as prisoners, but feasted them honorably. Mighty was the spoil and mighty great the booty. »

The fruit of this battle was the complete submission of the Pays de Vaud. Peter resumed possession of Moudon, Romont, and Morat, took Yverdon after a hard siege, and received the homage of Lausanne.

Then, according to the chronicle, he sent to Yverdon for the prisoners whom he had left at Chillon, Villeneuve, and elsewhere, and spoke to them as follows : « My Lord of Coppinguen, and you other lords, you have come to war against me; however God has favoured the right, since you are all my prisoners, as you see; know then that you have made me spend much money, and I should have good reasons to hold you at a high ransom, but I will not deal hardly. If then you, my lord of Coppinguen, will abandon to me the Pays de Vaud, without other ransom I will set you free. If not, you are not yet out of my hands, and I shall have the Pays de Vaud, whether you will or not. » Whereupon the Duke, though much it grieved him to lose such a jewel as the Pays de Vaud, replied : « I consent, provided I and mine be free and delivered. » — « As concerns you and your Germans, I will it be so », replied the Count, « but the lords of Vaud shall do me homage, and by their ransom shall aid me to bear my charges. » Nevertheless, after many words, all were set free, on condition of doing homage. Which being over, the Count sent for the ladies of the country to Yverdon, and especially those of the captive nobles, and feasted them during three days magnificently beyond all expression. »

The scene of hostilities, which had been prolonged in the vicinity of Fribourg and the Pays de Vaud, was now transported to the banks of the Aar; one by one the towns opened their gates, and all the barons of the country, as far as that river and the valleys of the Oberland, did homage for their possessions. Amid the acclamations of the citizens, Peter entered Berne, and was proclaimed its second founder. The only place in West Switzerland, which remained hostile to his authority, was Fribourg, but, while he was pressing the siege, overtures were made by Rodolph of Habsbourg, which resulted in a treaty of peace on conditions dictated by the Count of Savoy.

In the mean while, the Bishop of Sion having broken the truce, Peter hastened into the Valais, and was on the point of taking Sion by assault, when the Count and Bishop of Geneva interposed their mediation between the contending parties.

This was the last campaign of Count Peter. So constant a need of exertion had weakened his body and mind. He then retired to Chillon, to seek the repose which always eluded his grasp, and is said to have passed his latter days seeking, under that genial climate, to renovate his failing energies. Sometimes he passed his hours upon the lake, lulled by the gentle movement of the waves, and listening to the rhymes of his favorite troubadour Guillaume de Ferrato, or else, seated near the mighty hearth of the hall which still bears his name, he sought to reanimate the vital warmth diminished by the icy hand of age.

His career of activity ended at Chillon, but the home of his peaceful retreat did not witness his death, for he expired as he was returning there from a journey into Italy, June 12th 1268, and was buried among the princes of his house, at Haute Combe in Savoy.

Had he lived longer, he probably would have accomplished his object of forming a monarchy in West Switzerland, but neither he, nor his rival Rodolph of Habsbourg, succeeded in founding a firm dominion among the free born inhabitants of the Alps. It it strange that Peter should have bequeathed to history a name far less renowned than that of Rodolph, to whom he more than once proved himself superior. He is scarcely mentioned in the annals of England, and, in the country over which his rule extended, his memory, the object of an almost religious respect, floats in those vague regions between poetic fiction and historical detail, whence no image stands forth with precise and well ascertained features.

The Sack of La Tour. The house of Blonay.

The successors of Count Peter seldom made a long stay at Chillon, when they visited their dominions on this side the Alps. The marriage of Amedeus the Vth with Sybil of Baugé was celebrated there in 1272, in presence of Philip Count of Savoy and of the Bishop of Geneva.

The possession of the castle was entrusted to Governors, who rendered justice, received the prince's revenues, and commanded the garrison. During many years, this office was one of complete tranquillity, and the feudal halls had become a peaceful retirement, when in the month of June 1476, during the last contest between Charles the Bold of Burgundy, and the Swiss confederation, the banks of Montreux, and Chillon, again witnessed the disasters of war.

Amedeus of Gingins, Seigneur of Belmont in the province of Genevois, was then Captain general of the country about Chillon, and the head of the Lake. He was charged to watch the movements of the Valaisans, who had embraced the Swiss party, at the head of such militia of the country as had not followed the standard of the Count of Romont, on his march against Morat with the army of Charles of Burgundy. The better to fulfil his office, he had occupied a strong advanced position at St. Tryphon in the valley of the Rhone, leaving his brother Peter of Gingins, Seigneur of Chatelard, to command and guard Chillon with some troops from the neighbourhood.

The Bernese, by way of a diversion and in the hope of arresting the advance of the Duke of Burgundy, resolved on

sending aid to the Valaisans, and ordered Zurkinden, their
seneschal of the Upper Simmenthal, to enter the territory of
Vaud, at the head of 800 volunteers, by the valleys of Ges-
senay and of Chateau d'OEx, while 3000 Valaisans advanced
by the plain of the Rhone.

Zurkinden, after mustering his volunteers, on the night of
June 8th 1476, descended the pass of the Jaman, and, at
day break, appeared before the gates of La Tour, which he
found closed. The vigilance of Peter of Gingins had provided
against a surprise; the alarm had been given, and 400 trusty
vassals had arrived with him, resolved on defending the place
to the utmost. The little town was surrounded by a slight
wall, with a castle on the banks of the lake. Several assaults
were valiantly repulsed by the garrison, but the knight of
Chatelard, while setting a good example to his men, was
killed in the breach; upon this the garrison remained a mo-
ment, as if paralyzed, and the Bernese, seizing the occasion,
took the town and castle by storm. Neither age nor sex was
spared; old men, women, even children were put to the sword.
Eight men only survived the fury of the conquerors, and were
so fortunate as to escape by the Lake. After having passed
the night in riot and pillage, the Bernese set fire to La Tour,
and advanced on Vevey, which, being open to an enemy, ex-
perienced an almost similar fate.

In the mean time, the Valaisans were advancing down the
Rhone valley, where the knight of Belmont, at the head of a
small number of men, in vain strove to arrest their progress
at St. Tryphon. On learning the death of his brother, and the
destruction of La Tour, as he dared not venture on retreating
along the open plain, in presence of the superior forces of the
enemy, he crossed to the left bank of the Rhone, leaving the
road open for their passage before Chillon. The Valaisans
effected a junction with Zurkinden, and marched to Fribourg,
the rendez-vous of the allied troops, who, soon afterwards,
terminated the career of Charles the Bold at the battle of
Morat.

At the foot of the Pleiades, which terminate the chain of

the Alps, stands a small but ancient feudal castle, said to have been built as early as the tenth century. Its towers command a wide view over the Lake and mountains, and its owners formerly exercized supremacy over part of the town of Vevey and were Lords of more than twenty villages. Throughout the feudal ages, this family appear to have been firm adherents of the house of Savoy; one or two of the name held the post of seneschals of Chillon. Tradition relates that when the castle was taken by the Bernese, a Blonay, rather than abandon his liege lord and his faith, dashed on horseback into the lake, and, having escaped from the barks which were pressing the castle on the water side, swam to the opposite bank, where he was received with rare distinction by Duke Charles IIIrd of Savoy. A branch of the family then settled on the South side of the lake, but the main stem, who remained in the Canton de Vaud, though they jealously and courteously defended their rights, inch by inch, were compelled at last to pay homage to the Bernese conquerors, and gradually descended from their knightly state into the condition of private gentlemen. The castle, which has been transmitted with a moderate surrounding property from father to son, is inhabited by the present representative of the ancient house.

A chronicle, contained in the archives of Turin, relates how, some years before the Duke Charles IIIrd of Savoy lost the territory of Vaud, several gentlemen, youths, and esquires had met at a banquet of the court. Some of them were married, some single. After many joyous devices and amusements, they began to compare their respective conditions; when Simon de Blonay, who had bowed beneath the gentle yoke of marriage, declared plainly that the married men were as juvenile, and as doughty champions as the bachelors; likewise that the married ladies were as worthy of praise and renown as the unmarried, and this he offered to maintain with lance and sword against any gainsayer.

Thereupon, for the bachelors and maidens, stood forth the knight of Corsant in the country of Bresse. The Duke, seeing no malice was intended, consented to a combat, two courses on horseback with ground lances, and fifteen sword strokes, on condition that the vanquished, if the champion of the married, should cry mercy, first of the Princess of Savoy, then of whatever noble maiden the conqueror should name; if the advocate of the unmarried, he should bend the knee before the Duchess of Savoy, then should go and kneel to the wife of the knight of Blonay.

On the 12th of May 1504, the combatants appeared before the castle of Turin; De Blonay on a grey charger, steel caparisoned, wearing red and black favours; Corsant on a piebald, with grey and crimson colours. At the first encounter, the success was evenly balanced, and the lances of both burst into shivers. Each received a fresh lance, when De Blonay broke his weapon against his adversary's breast, so fair and forcibly that armour, saddle, and horseman were borne to the earth with such violence that many thought the poor knight was dead. But quickly Corsant rose to his feet, ready to renew the combat sword in hand.

The laws of the tournament did not allow him who was unhorsed to mount again before the end of the combat; but De Blonay courteously waived the question. The struggle was renewed on horseback with the sword; innumerable were the cuts and thrusts, given and received with equal gallantry; when the Duke of Savoy, that it might not be carried too far, gave orders to stay their strokes, and adjudged the honor of the day to the married knight.

The author then concludes the adventure. After a short repose, Corsant, according to the terms of the combat, went to cry mercy on both knees of the Lady of Savoy, and as much, with one knee to the ground, of all the other married ladies of the palace. Then he begged to know of the knight of Blonay where he should find his noble dame, that he might go to her, to pay his debt and ask pardon. « Loyal and gallant champion », Blonay answered him, « I cannot in faith well say where now is my lady and well beloved, whom I left in childbed on the other side the mountains; but either she is in

Chablais at my castle of St. Paul of Meillerie, or at my castle of Blonay in Vaud. »

« Then , though the way was long and dangerous, forthwith Corsant, mounted on a good steed and followed by his squire, in great haste passed the mountains. First he came to the castle of Meillerie ; but the lady not being there, speedily he took a fisher's boat, and, though night was falling , made for Vevey, where the rough weather on the Lake did not permit him to land before the dawn, but though sore weary, he mounted straight to the castle of Blonay. Then, the first person he saw was the noble dame Catherine , on the lawn, nursing her fair infant. Having approached, he quickly bent his knee, and thrice cried mercy most piteously. Who was then astonished and in great alarm but the dame of Blonay ! Speedily she made him rise, and take seat by her side ; then, all in wonder, enquired what that meant. Corsant related to her all the adventure, and how, having been vanquished by her courteous husband, he was fulfilling the law of the combat, and required quittance for his honor, and discharge. »

Whereon the lady said to him with a gentle voice : « Sir champion of the unmarried , an honorable and free hearted knight are you in truth, and certes no one will gainsay it : however it beseemeth not a discreet and prudent dame, left solitary in her manor house, to receive you in absence of her husband. Return then to Vevey ; take your repose and night's lodging, and tomorrow, if so please you, about noon, return to seek your quittance and leave to depart. » As she said, so did he.

And he failed not on the morrow to arrive at midday. The banquet was prepared in the great hall of the castle , even many relatives and neighbours of the noble dame, invited in great haste , were there present ; towit the Lord Anthony of Gruyère , come from his castle of Oron , with squires and pages, Sir Humbert of Aubonne her godfather, Hugonet of Chatelard, Nicod of Goumoëns, Amedeus of Puidoux, Bertrand of Duyn seneschal of Chillon, and the chaplain old Anselm of Tavel. The banquet was long and joyous , according to the

good custom of Vaud ; so that the sun , at his setting , saw
them still feasting and holding joyous converse. Each listened
to Corsant, who happened not to be known to any of the
noble company, and who gained the esteem of all by his good
favour, his gentle language and his courtesy. Each questioned
him, now upon the combat, now of other subjects beyond the
mountains. The banquet drawing to an end, he rose, and pro-
posing the health of the noble dame : « It is not to my loss,
said he, so much as to my gain, that I have been worsted in
my combat with the knight your husband ; for never had I
such honour and joy as this day, sitting with company of so
high lineage. Thus do I advance towards the fulfilment of my
motto : « altius » (upwards). In consequence my mind is, that
I must directly take wife, and that then I shall better maintain
the cause of the married, than I have upheld that of the un-
married at the combat of Turin. » And so saying, he turned
gently towards Yolande of Villette , who was seated by the
dame of Blonay, her cousin. A fair young maiden was she,
and of good birth : but alas ! an orphan, having neither dower,
nor estate in this world , she had come to take her leave
before entering the cloister of the nuns of Orbe. Soon as the
knight had fixed his gaze a moment on her, the poor soul
became red as scarlet, and uttered nothing but a deep sigh.

And when they quitted the table, each made ready to
depart ; Corsant, remaining till the last, as if to express his
thanks to the dame of Blonay, began to say to her : « Courtesy
is yours, as much as beauty; I have a request to make of
you, grant it me, if you wish me well. » — « Speak, answered
the noble lady, and if it exceeds not my means and duty, I
feel sure we shall accomplish your desire. » — « It is, said Cor-
sant, that you plead my cause with your fair cousin, in order
that henceforth I may have right to maintain the cause of the
married, for, soon as I saw her, I made of her the lady of my
thoughts, and so shall she be until my death. » — The fair cou-
sin, who was not far off, cast down her blue eyes, and the
lady said : « If I understand rightly, you would fain become
my cousin , it is not so, fair Sir ? If the young maiden is of

my mind, she will absolve you from all blame, and soon make of you a good husband instead of a sad young man as you are. »

Hearing such talk, the poor Yolande knew not in what corner to hide for very shame. But the acquaintance was made, inasmuch as Mother Nature had already shaken the sparks of love's torch over those young hearts. So well that at last, Yolande, without thinking more of the cloister than if cloister never had existed, said in a low voice : « Yes, if my cousin Sir Simon, who is my guardian, makes no objection. »

Sir Simon, who arrived four days later, did not gainsay the gentle cousin. He even held their wedding feast in his castle of Blonay. And Corsant said to him : « Noble cousin, I have lost nought in being vanquished by you ; thence I have gained for my lot a good and fair wife, and if any one now should speak against the married men, I will take cause in hand, and treat him as you did me at the combat of Turin. »

Such is a faithful picture of the manners of the feudal nobility of Vaud, in the last days of the house of Savoy.

About the year 1595, the family of Blonay had increased their domains by the acquisition of the castle of Chatelard, and its territory, which extended from the woody slopes of mount Cubli to the orchards of Clarens. This residence was generally the property of the younger branches of the family.

About 1640, the daughter of the baron of Chatelard, Barbille Nicolaide de Blonay, was renowned for her surpassing beauty. An officer in the French service, De Tavel of Villars, obtained, as the reward of several years' persevering courtship, the promise of her hand, which many young gentlemen had sought in vain. During his absence on military duties, and, although an affectionate correspondence was carried on between the betrothed couple, Jean François de Blonay, knight of Bernex, of the Catholic and Savoyard branch of the family, took advantage of his visits to Chatelard as a relative, to gain the young lady's heart. He ventured on asking her hand, which was refused him by the parents as already promised. Then, backed by the influence of the Duchess of Savoy, he renewed his demand with the same ill success. At last. resolved on attaining by foul means what had been refused to his prayers, he concealed himself with some friends in the environs of Chatelard, and, taking advantage of a moment when the young lady was alone unguarded in the castle, carried her off, January 9th 1642, crossed the lake, and became her husband.

The noise of this abduction caused great agitation on both sides of the lake. The baron of Chatelard, though rather indifferent to the matter, made his complaint before the Court of Savoy. De Tavel deeply felt the injury, and a legal process was commenced at Berne. The influence of the Courts of France and Savoy had great weight there in favour of the De Blonays, who wished to spread the veil of oblivion over the complaint of the adverse party. De Tavel secured the assistance of his relative, General d'Erlach de Castelen, the independent commander of a large body of mercenaries. Through his influence, a judgment was pronounced in favour of De Tavel. Jean François de Blonay, and the two friends who had assisted him, were declared traitors, and their goods forfeit to the State of Berne; they were summoned to restore the lady to her father's castle, and condemned to pay to De Tavel an indemnity of about L. 700 by way of consolation. The Baron of Chatelard was severely reprimanded for negligence in execution of his paternal duties. This sentence however remained a dead letter, as none of the parties except the Baron of Chatelard were within the jurisdiction of the court; nevertheless, the government of Berne, by this means, gave all the satisfaction they could to their own honour, as well as to the urgent solicitations of the General d'Erlach; De Tavel remained a melancholy warning to future bachelors, that he, who leaves his intended too long in solitude for the sake of gathering laurels, may chance to wear the willow.

The Reform. Bonivard. The Bernese Bailiffs.

At the beginning of the 16th century, the house of Savoy still possessed, on both sides of the lake, a territory nearly as extensive in appearance as in the days of Peter, the little Charlemagne. In reality a total change had taken place. Amedeus the VIIIth, on becoming Pope Felix Vth, had incurred great debts, which proved an endless burden to his successors, and were mortgaged on their best revenues, among others on Chillon. The ducal sceptre had passed into the hands of feeble princes, women, and minors. Above all, the ruin of Charles of Burgundy had greatly weakened his allies the princes of Savoy, and the Swiss had ravaged the Pays de Vaud. The Bernese and Fribourgeois had seized on several important places, and extended their possessions to the Rhone.

To shew the anarchy of the times, we may add that, upon slight causes of quarrel, one town made war on another; the mountaineers often descended into the plain to pillage hamlets, and carry off the vintage. Occasionally some chief of mercenary bands, pretending to be a creditor of the Duke of Savoy, and that it was impossible otherwise to obtain payment of his claim, levied men and seized on the place which, as he represented, was mortgaged to him. Thus one Scharnacthal fixed himself at Chillon, and would not quit the castle, until he had exhausted the last resources of its territory.

While, on one side, the Duke of Savoy and his adherents fulminated at Moudon an anathema against Martin Luther, on the other, Berne and most of the important towns of Switzerland had received the Reform with open arms.

During this period of agitation, a distinguished character paved the way for the Reform and liberty at Geneva. Francis Bonivard was a Savoyard of noble family; born at Seyssel in 1494, he was allied by ties of relationship to the chief nobles of the country. His education was completed at Turin, with the exception of a short period passed at Fribourg in Brisgau. By the bequest of an uncle, in his twentieth year, he became

3

Prior of St. Victor, a small monastery situate in the suburb of Geneva, and no sooner had he entered on his post, than from conviction he devoted his energies to the perilous task of promoting the liberties of that city.

This line of conduct rendered him obnoxious to the Duke of Savoy, between whose partizans, and the friends of liberty, a perpetual agitation was kept up in Geneva. One day, a relative of Bonivard's, who had just arrived from Turin, proposed to him, as a means of regaining the Duke's favor, to betray some of the head men of the liberal party, and deliver them to him bound hand and foot. Not only did Bonivard decline this offer indignantly, but, by his courageous interposition, he saved from death a patriot who had been tortured, and was about to be executed by sentence of the Bishop of Geneva. Then he tranquilly retired to his convent, where, says he, « I felt such youthful presumption and vain arrogance, that I feared neither Duke, nor Bishop, and God gave me there such good fortune that, for the moment, they could not hurt me. »

His position was a painful one; an outcast, in consequence of his liberal ideas, from the society of the nobles to which he belonged, and unable to feel a sound esteem or friendship for those to whom he had extended a helping hand. The unbridled riotous license of the populace, the petty details of political intrigue, the selfishness of the rich tradesmen, were repulsive to the enlightened sentiments of the well educated man of generous mind, who had formed his idea of liberty from the grand conceptions of the ancients, or the kindly precepts of the Gospel.

In his character and writings appear many contradictory qualities, a careless lightness of heart, an original vein of irony, a sceptical turn for enquiry, but a devoted attachment to the cause he had embraced; he had read much, and reasons acutely.

His incessant endeavours, to form a close alliance between Geneva and the Swiss Cantons, rendered him peculiarly obnoxious to Charles IIIrd of Savoy. On hearing that the Duke was about to visit the city, he deemed it prudent to retire for a while, and, disguised as a monk, he set out for the territory of the Cantons, under the guidance of two false friends, a gentleman and an abbot, who, on the way, extorted from him by threats the cession of his monastery of St. Victor, and then delivered him to the Duke, at whose hands he underwent a first captivity of two years at Gex.

On regaining his liberty, as the usurping Abbot was dead, and the discomfiture of the Pope, at the sack of Rome by the Constable of Bourbon, had caused a complete anarchy in ecclesiastical affairs, he applied to the Bishop of Geneva, his friend and relative, who restored him to his monastery.

But the grand point was to recover its revenues, and the small castle of Cartigny which commanded the domain. Boni-vard then made war upon a small scale on his own account, took the castle, and placed therein a garrison of six men under a captain, who allowed it to be surprized in his absence. Upon this he made an agreement with a Bernese butcher, who, with some other adventurers, undertook to put him in posses-sion of his castle; the little army was defeated after a short campaign, and Bonivard, unable to dispose of his convent in exchange for a small pension, was reduced to a state of poverty by no means in accordance with his former fortune and rank.

The cause of the Reform now made great progress at Ge-neva, and Bonivard became one of its warmest partizans; but, strange to say, in spite of the animosity which he might na-turally suppose that his conduct had excited in the mind of the Duke of Savoy, he ventured on addressing that prince for assistance, and offered to sell him the Priory of St. Victor.

His mother, who lived at Seyssel in Savoy, was ill and kept her bed; therefore a safe conduct for a month was gran-ted him by the Duke, to visit her, and discuss the question of the sale of his rights.

This safe conduct was prolonged for the month of May, during which he resolved on visiting Fribourg. There he found the marshal of Savoy and other men of note, who gave him every assurance of reconciliation with the Duke. From Fri-bourg he visited the Bishop at Lausanne, and thence went to

Moudon, where an important audience was being held concerning the affairs of the Count of Gruyère. He was favorably received by the persons in authority, and the Duchess' steward furnished him a horse and guide for his return to Lausanne. But as soon as they were near St. Catherine on the Jorat, he was attacked by Antoine de Beaufort, Governor of Chillon, who with several companions had lain in wait for him in a wood. Before he had time to draw his sword, he was seized and disarmed, his own guide being the first to set on him. In spite of the safe conduct, he was arrested in the Duke's name and carried off, bound hand and foot, to Chillon.

Bonivard himself gives few details of his captivity. The pillar is shewn to which he is said to have been fastened, as well as the ring which held his chain. He informs us in his chronicles, that he was not at first confined in the dungeon, but, during two years, was lodged in a chamber near that of the Governor, who frequently visited and shewed him much kindness. The two gentlemen related their adventures to each other ; the Governor affected much openness of manner, and endeavoured to attach Bonivard as a partizan to the Duke's interest. That Prince however made a visit to Chillon, and put an end to the previous good treatment of the prisoner. « Then, says he, the Captain thrust me into a cell lower than the lake, where I lived four years ; I know not whether he did it by the Duke's order, or of his own accord ; but sure it is that I had so much leisure for walking, that I wore in the rock, which was the pavement, a track or little path, as if it had been made with a hammer. »

While the hours were passing wearily with Bonivard in his dungeon, the aspect of affairs had greatly changed on the banks of the lake. The Duke had for several years blockaded Geneva, the town was hard pressed, and its inhabitants, after long solicitations, had persuaded the Bernese to send an army of 6000 men to their assistance in February 1536. The troops set forth chaunting a war song of which the conclusion was : « In this age of sorrow for the children of God, of struggles for the poor in heart, the bear, the bear alone, has

opened its heart to pity. Up then, my valiant beast, and woe
to whomever does not arm like thee to fight the hypocrites and
canting rogues. »

Their advance sufficed, without opposition, to disperse the
few troops the Duke of Savoy could set on foot, and to con-
quer the Pays de Vaud ; but the soldiers, desirous of returning
home with the fruits of their pillage, quitted the campaign
before the work was completed. The Captain of Chillon arro-
gantly continued his predatory excursions on the shores of the
lake, despoiling all he could lay hands on.

The Bernese republic then resolved on sending a thousand
men, under the command of Nægueli, to complete their con-
quest, and especially to reduce Chillon. The Genevese, who
had refused to make peace with the Duke of Savoy, unless he
liberated Bonivard and abandoned his claim on the convent of
St. Victor, were invited to second the Bernese in arms.

Two armed galleys, two barks, and some smaller vessels
set out for the attack, manned by all the adventurous spirits
of Geneva. On arriving in the upper part of the Lake, they
cruised there some time, in expectation of news of the arrival
of the Bernese. At last a distant cannon shot gave the signal
of their having reached Lutry, and, a few hours later, Chillon
was invested.

The garrison consisted of some Italian troops, and vassals
of the neighbourhood, under De Beaufort. On the eve of the
29th of March 1536, the trenches were opened against the castle.
The next day, the Bernese commenced their fire from the land
side, while the Genevese galleys battered it from the Lake. At
nightfall the Governor demanded a parley, as he was short of
provisions, and feared, in case of a successful assault, to
undergo the ruthless treatment, by which the Bernese had
generally signalized themselves. He offered to capitulate, if
allowed to retire with the garrison, their arms, and baggage.
The Bernese would only grant these terms for him and the
Italian soldiers, claiming the rest as their own subjects.

During the parley, De Beaufort with most part of the gar-
rison, his wife, and three chests of treasure, which had been

deposited at Chillon, as the most secure stronghold, by parties from even ten leagues around, contrived to get on board a large bark anchored under the castle wall. He passed adroitly between the Genevese galleys, and made for La Tour Ronde on the coast of Savoy, where, being hard pursued, he hastily threw his cannon overboard, set fire to his vessel, and escaped with the treasure into the mountains of the Chablais.

An ancient legend relates that, on quitting the castle, De Beaufort buried his riches in the cemetery, and now returns at midnight to count it over.

Deprived of his presence, the castle surrendered about noon, and the Bernese rushed into the interior. In the dungeon, Bonivard was found chained to the pillar, and his first question, on learning his own restoration to liberty, was whether Geneva had gained her freedom also. Three other prisoners were in the castle, one of whom, a Savoyard gentleman named d'Arbignon, had been lodged there on the charge of having murdered his own servant for some little money he knew the man to possess. The Duke had given orders to have all the captives put to death, but this, the Governor, for fear of the Bernese, had not dared to do. The gentleman, whom Bonivard styles Barabbas, was tried for the murder, and being found guilty, was executed by order of the allies.

After his captivity, Bonivard composed several works in prose and poetry, the chief of these are, his Chronicles of Geneva, a poem on the Origin of evil, and some satirical verse, in which he vents his indignation against the hypocrisy of the Popes, and the petty tyrant Charles the IIIrd of Savoy.

The citizens of Geneva were by no means backward in recompensing him for past sufferings; in June 1536 he was admitted to the highest civic honours, and presented with the house previously inhabited by the Roman Catholic Vicar General, besides an annual pension of 200 gold crowns. The fair sex appear to have been by no means insensible to his merits, as he married no less than four times without being blest with children, and an order of the state is said to be extant, enjoining the removal from his residence of an ambitious housekeeper who, in his old age, was near persuading him to promote her to the upper end of his board. Since he was through life careless about money matters, the city of Geneva watched with tender solicitude over his declining years, paid his debts, examined the justice of his creditors' claims, and allowed no imposition to be practised on him. When suffering from severe illness, the town council removed him from his house, which they considered too hot, and had him conveyed into an apartment in the Hotel de Ville, until complete recovery. He ended his days in peace, and his memory is revered by the Genevese, as that of a martyr to their liberty,

The view of the place of his captivity suggested to Byron the idea of « the Prisoner of Chillon », which he wrote during four days rainy weather at the Hotel de l'Ancre at Ouchy ; the details of the poem are entirely fictitious, and do not relate to the history of Bonivard.

The conquest of Chillon ensured the possession of all the Canton de Vaud to the Bernese. A Bailiff, with the title of « Captain of Chillon », took the place of the former Seneschals. The first was Augustin de Luternau ; his authority extended over the district of Vevey and Villeneuve.

When Emanuel Philibert of Savoy, had, in 1557, gained the decisive battle of St. Quentin against the French, and had ascended the throne of his ancestors, he demanded restitution of the territory held by Berne on both sides of the lake. In him the Swiss would doubtless have met a formidable adversary, and they consented readily to restore the South side. The Duke demanded the surrender of the whole, offering to pay them 140,000 crowns in discharge of the debts of his grandfather Charles IIIrd, and to rase Chillon. The Bernese preferred the hazards of war to compliance with his demand, but at length a treaty was made at Nyon in 1564 , by which the Duke gave up his claim to Chillon.

Twenty four years later, says an ancient author, the Duke Charles Emanuel of Savoy renewed his claim to the Pays de Vaud. The nobility of the country had joined in a conspiracy

for the deliverance of Lausanne and the chief places on the
lake into his hands. Two flotillas were advancing, one to-
wards Ouchy, the other towards Chillon. Among the conspi-
rators was a gentleman of Villeneuve, named Bouvier, lieute-
nant of the Bailiff of Chillon, who had undertaken to surprise
the castle. For that purpose he had posted men in ambush in the
neighbouring forest, and had gone to dine with the unsuspec-
ting Bailiff. While they were at table, a letter arrived dis-
closing the discovery of the conspiracy. The Bailiff read it
hastily and, turning to his guest, said : « I am sorry, friend,
but I have orders to arrest you. » Bouvier, caught in his own
snare, begged for two hours respite to put his household in
order. The Bailiff, an open hearted man, allowed him to go to
Villeneuve under good escort. Near his house door was the
entrance of the cellar, and the custom of the country was
then, as now in many places, to shew friends into the cellar
and take refreshment there, nor were the guards so hardhear-
ted as to refuse the prisoner that consolation. They tasted
first of one wine barrel, then of another, each better than the
preceding; when they had arrived at the best of all, Bouvier
made his escape through a trap door, locked the soldiers in,
and, after packing up his valuables, rode off, forded the
Rhone, and reached Savoy in safety.

Under the Bernese government, the reign of severe morality
was installed as the law of the land. In 1652 orders were
sent to the Captain of Chillon to find out those suspected of
witchcraft, and, at three different times, on three different
days, in presence of two sworn and experienced persons, to
search for the marks of Satan. In consequence three victims,
a man and two women, were burnt alive.

Lewdness, drunkenness, gluttony, baptismal and burial
feasts, tobacco, idleness, self conceit and dancing were then
prohibited under severe penalties. The length of wigs was
regulated by law ; the wearing of false hair, or of more than
one petticoat, was absolutely forbidden. Short sleeves and
low dresses were the objects of repeated fulminations, and
great wrath, says Vuillemin, was once excited in the heart

of their Excellencies of Berne at the news that a Roman Catholic dancing master had established himself in their good town of Vevey, and caused great scandal, even balls by night, whereat both sexes were present. Order was sent to the Bailiff of Chillon to make him speedily decamp, and to censure the town's people for their criminal laxity.

Although this period is looked back upon by the natives of the country as one of humiliation under the Bernese yoke, yet to its effects, and to the stern principles of morality inculcated by force at that epoch, may be attributed the intellectual development and industrious habits of the Pays de Vaud, whence arises the marked superiority of its inhabitants over those of the territory restored to Savoy.

The Bailiffs were invariably the benefactors of the poor. Vuillemin relates how in 1712, when incessant rains had rotted the crops, Vincent Frisching distributed among the indigent the stores of corn hoarded up in the granaries of the state, how he daily left the castle to visit the needy, to enquire into their wants, and cheer them by his sympathy. When the lake had fallen six feet, and the streams had been exhausted, in the droughts of 1713 and 1714, the same man continued his acts of unwearied beneficence, and shared his very bread with the poor.

In 1733, the seat of the Bailiff's government was transferred to Vevey, where it remained, until the French revolution encouraged the Vaudois to rise in arms against the Bernese in January 1798.

The castle was seized by the inhabitants of Vevey and Montreux without bloodshed. It had long been employed as a prison for political offenders, and when, in 1803, the Pays de Vaud was raised to the rank of the 19th Canton of Switzerland, it was converted into an arsenal for the artillery and a place of detention for criminals.

Such is its present destination, and, although its walls have been much defaced by application of white wash, Chillon still remains the most interesting historical monument on the banks of the Lake, and has not lost its original stamp of antiquity.

—o-o-oo◁◖O◗▷oo-o-o—

THE PRISONER OF CHILLON.

Eternal spirit ot the chainless mind!
  Brightest in dungeons, Liberty! thou art,
  For there thy habitation is the heart—
The heart which love of thee alone can bind;
And when thy sons to fetters are consign'd—
  To fetters, and the damp vault's dayless gloom,
  Their country conquers with their martyrdom,
And Freedom's fame finds wings on every wind.
Chillon! thy prison is a holy place,
  And thy sad floor an altar—for't was trod,
Until his very steps have left a trace
  Worn, as if thy cold pavement were a sod,
By Bonivard! — May none those marks efface!
For they appeal from Tyranny to God.

My hair is grey, but not with years,
  Nor grew it white
  In a single night,
As men's have grown from sudden fears;
My limbs are bow'd, though not with toil,
  But rusted with a vile repose,
For they have been a dungeon's spoil,
  And mine has been the fate of those
To whom the goodly earth and air
Are bann'd, and barr'd—forbidden fare :
But this was for my father's faith,
I suffer'd chains and courted death.
That father perish'd at the stake

For tenets he would not forsake;
And for the same his lineal race
In darkness found a dwelling-place.
We were seven—who now are one;
   Six in youth, and one in age,
Finish'd as they had begun,
   Proud of Persecution's rage;
One in fire, and two in field,
Their belief with blood have seal'd,
Dying as their father died,
For the God their foes denied :
Three were in a dungeon cast,
Of whom this wreck is left the last.

There are seven pillars of Gothic mould,
In Chillon's dungeons deep and old;
There are seven columns, massy and grey,
Dim with a dull imprison'd ray,
A sunbeam which hath lost its way,
And through the crevice and the cleft
Of the thick wall is fallen and left,
Creeping o'er the floor so damp,
Like a marsh's meteor-lamp :
And in each pillar there is a ring,
   And in each ring there is a chain;
That iron is cankering thing,
   For in these limbs its teeth remain,
With marks that will not wear away,
Till I have done with this new day,
Which now is painful to these eyes,
Which have not seen the sun so rise
For years—I cannot count them o'er;
I lost their long and heavy score
When my last brother droop'd and died,
And I lay living by his side.

They chain'd us each to a column stone,
And we were three—yet, each alone;
We could not move a single pace,
We could not see each other's face,
But with that pale and livid light
That made us strangers in our sight :

And thus together—yet apart,
Fetter'd in hand, but pined in heart,
'T was still some solace in the dearth
Of the pure elements of earth,
To hearken to each other's speech,
And each turn comforter to each
With some new hope, or legend old,
Or song heroically bold;
But even these at length grew cold:
Our voices took a dreary tone,
An echo of the dungeon stone,
  A grating sound—not full and free
  As they of yore were wont to be:
  It might be fancy—but to me
They never sounded like our own.

I was the eldest of the three,
  And to uphold and cheer the rest
  I ought to do—and did my best—
And each did well in his degree.
  The youngest, whom my father loved,
Because our mother's brow was given
To him—with eyes as blue as heaven,
  For him my soul was sorely moved;
And truly might it be distress'd
To see such bird in such a nest.
For he was beautiful as day—
  (When day was beautiful to me
  As to young eagles, being free)—
  A polar day, which will not see
A sunset till its summer 's gone,
  Its sleepless summer of long light,
The snow-clad offspring of the sun!
  And thus he was as pure and bright,
And in his natural spirit gay,
With tears for nought but other's ills,
And then they flow'd like mountain rills,
Unless he could assuage the woe
Which he abhorr'd to view below.

The other was as pure of mind,
But form'd to combat with his kind;
Strong in his frame, and of a mood

Which 'gainst the world in war had stood,
And perish'd in the foremost rank
  With joy :—but not in chains to pine :
His spirit wither'd with their clank,
  I saw it silently decline—
And so perchance in sooth did mine;
But yet I forced it on to cheer
Those relics of a home so dear.
He was a hunter of the hills,
  Had follow'd there the deer and wolf;
To him this dungeon was a gulf,
And fetter'd feet the worst of ills.

  Lake Leman lies by Chillon's walls :
A thousand feet in depth below
Its massy waters meet and flow;
Thus much the fathom-line was sent
From Chillon's snow-white battlement,
  Which round about the wave inthrals.
A double dungeon wall and wave
Have made—and like a living grave.
Below the surface of the lake
The dark vault lies wherein we lay;
We heard it ripple night and day;
  Sounding o'er our heads it knock'd;
And I have felt the winter's spray
Wash through the bars when winds were high
And wanton in the happy sky;
  And then the very rock hath rock'd,
  And I have felt it shake, unshock'd,
Because I could have smiled to see
The death that would have set me free.

I said my nearer brother pined,
I said his mighty heart declined,
He loathed and put away his food.
It was not that 't was coarse and rude;
For we were used to hunter's fare,
And for the like had little care :
The milk drawn from the mountain goat
Was changed for water from the moat,
Our bread was such as captive's tears

Have moisten'd many a thousand years,
Since man first pent his fellow men
Like brutes within an iron den :
But what were these to us or him?
These wasted not his heart or limb;
My brother's soul was of that mould
Which in a palace had grown cold,
Had his free breathing been denied
The range of the steep mountain's side;
But why delay the truth?—he died.
I saw, and could not hold his head
Nor reach his dying hand—nor dead,—
Though hard I strove, but strove in vain
To rend and gnash my bonds in twain.
He died—and they unlock'd his chain,
And scoop'd for him a shallow grave
Even from the cold earth of our cave.
I begg'd them, as a boon, to lay
His corse in dust whereon the day
Might shine—it was a foolish thought,
But then within my brain it wrought,
That even in death his freeborn breast
In such a dungeon could not rest.
I might have spared my idle prayer—
They coldly laugh'd—and laid him there :
The flat and turfless earth above
The being we so much did love ;
His empty chain above it leant,
Such murder's fitting monument!

But he, the favourite and the flower,
Most cherish'd since his natal hour,
His mother's image in fair face,
The infant love of all his race,
His martyr'd father's dearest thought,
My latest care, for whom I sought
To hoard my life, that his might be
Less wretched now, and one day free,
He, too, who yet had held untired
A spirit natural or inspired—
He, too, was struck, and day by day
Was wither'd on the stalk away.

Oh God! it is a fearful thing
To see the human soul take wing
In any shape, in any mood :—
I 've seen it rushing forth in blood,
I 've seen it on the breaking ocean
Strive with a swoln convulsive motion,
I 've seen the sick and ghastly bed
Of Sin delirious with its dread :
But these were horrors—this was woe
Unmix'd with such—but sure and slow.
He faded, and so calm and meek,
So softly worn, so sweetly weak,
So tearless, yet so tender—kind,
And grieved for those he left behind;
With all the while a cheek whose bloom
Was as a mockery of the tomb,
Whose tints as gently sunk away
As a departing rainbow's ray—
An eye of most transparent light,
That almost made the dungeon bright;
And not a word of murmur—not
A groan o'er his untimely lot,—
A little talk of better days,
A little hope my own to raise,
For I was sunk in silence—lost
In this last loss, of all the most.
And then the sighs he would suppress
Of fainting nature's feebleness,
More slowly drawn, grew less and less :
I listen'd, but I could not hear—
I call'd, for I was wild with fear;
I knew 't was hopeless, but my dread
Would not be thus admonished;
I call'd, and thought I heard a sound—
I burst my chain with one strong bound,
And rush'd to him :—I found him not,
I only stirr'd in this black spot,
I only lived—I only drew
The accursed breath of dungeon-dew;
The last—the sole—the dearest link
Between me and the eternal brink,
Which bound me to my failing race,

Was broken in this fatal place.
One on the earth, and one beneath—
My brothers—both had ceased to breathe.
I took that hand which lay so still,
Alas! my own was full as chill;
I had not strength to stir, or strive,
But felt that I was still alive—
A frantic feeling, when we know
That what we love shall ne'er be so.
    I know not why
    I could not die;
I had no earthly hope—but faith,
And that forbade a selfish death. ·
What next befell me then and there
   I know not well—I never knew—
First came the loss of light, and air,
   And then of darkness too.
I had no thought, no feeling—none—
Among the stones I stood a stone,
And was scarce conscious what I wist,
As shrubless crags within the mist;
For all was blank, and bleak, and gray,—
It was not night—it was not day,
It was not even the dungeon-light,
So hateful to my heavy sight,
But vacancy absorbing space,
And fixedness—without a place;
There were no stars—no earth—no time—
No check—no change—no good—no crime
But silence, and a stirless breath
Which neither was of life nor death;
A sea of stagnant idleness,
Blind, boundless, mute, and motionless!

A light broke in upon my brain,—
   It was the carol of a bird;
It ceased, and then it came again,
   The sweetest song ear ever heard,
And mine was thankful till my eyes
Ran over with the glad surprise,
And they that moment could not see
I was the mate of misery;

But then by dull degrees came back
My senses to their wonted track :
I saw the dungeon walls and floor
Close slowly round me as before,
I saw the glimmer of the sun
Creeping as it before had done;
But through the crevice where it came
That bird was perch'd, as fond and tame,
 And tamer than upon the tree;
A lovely bird, with azure wings,
And song that said a thousand things,
 And seem'd to say them all for me!
I never saw its like before,
I ne'er shall see its likeness more :
It seem'd like me to want a mate,
But was not half so desolate;
And it was come to love me when
None lived to love me so again,
And cheering from my dungeon's brink
Had brought me back to feel and think.
I know not if it late were free,
 Or broke its cage to perch on mine,
But knowing well captivity,
Sweet bird! I could not wish for thine!
Or if it were, in winged guise,
A visitant from Paradise;
For—Heaven forgive that thought! the while
Which made me both to weep and smile—
I sometimes deem'd that it might be
My brother's soul come down to me;
But then at last away it flew,
And then 't was mortal—well I knew,
For he would never thus have flown,
And left me twice so doubly lone,—
Lone—as the corse within its shroud,
Lone—as a solitary cloud,
 A single cloud on a sunny day,
While all the rest of heaven is clear,
A frown upon the atmosphere,
That hath no business to appear
 When skies are blue, and earth is gay.

4

A kind of change came in my fate;
My keepers grew compassionate.
I know not what had made them so;
They were inured to sights of woe :
But so it was :—my broken chain
With links unfasten'd did remain,
And it was liberty to stride
Along my cell from side to side,
And up and down, and then athwart,
And tread it over every part;
And round the pillars one by one,
Returning where my walk begun,
Avoiding only, as I trod,
My brothers' graves without a sod;
For if I thought with heedless tread
My step profaned their lowly bed,
My breath came gaspingly and thick,
And my crush'd heart fell blind and sick.
I made a footing in the wall,—
It was not therefrom to escape,
For I had buried one and all
Who loved me in a human shape;
And the whole earth would henceforth be
A wider prison unto me :
No child—no sire—no kin had I,
No partner in my misery;
I thought of this, and I was glad,
For thought of them had made me mad;
But I was curious to ascend
To my barr'd windows, and to bend
Once more, upon the mountains high,
The quiet of a loving eye.

I saw them—and they were the same,
They were not changed like me in frame;
I saw their thousand years of snow
On high—their wide long lake below,
And the blue Rhone in fullest flow;
I heard the torrents leap and gush
O'er channell'd rock and broken bush;
I saw the white-wall'd distant town,
And whiter sails go skimming down;

And then there was a little isle,
Which in my very face did smile,
  The only one in view,
A small green isle, it seem'd no more,
Scarce broader than my dungeon-floor,
But in it there were three tall trees,
And o'er it blew the mountain breeze,
And by it there were waters flowing,
And on it there were young flowers growing,
  Of gentle breath and hue.
The fish swam by the castle-wall,
And they seem'd joyous each and all;
The eagle rode the rising blast,
Methought he never flew so fast
As then to me he seem'd to fly—
And then new tears came in my eye,
And I felt troubled—and would fain
I had not left my recent chain;
And when I did descend again,
The darkness of my dim abode
Fell on me as a heavy load;
It was as is a new-dug grave,
Closing o'er one we sought to save,—
And yet my glance, too much oppress'd,
Had almost need of such a rest.

It might be months, or years, or days,
  I kept no count—I took no note,
I had no hope my eyes to raise,
  And clear them of their dreary mote;
At last men came to set me free,
I ask'd not why, and reck'd not where,
It was at length the same to me,
Fetter'd or fetterless to be:
  I learn'd to love despair.
And thus when they appear'd at last,
And all my bonds aside were cast,
These heavy walls to me had grown
A hermitage—and all my own!
And half I felt as they were come
To tear me from a second home:
With spiders I had friendship made,

And watch'd them in their sullen trade,
Had seen the mice by moonlight play,
And why should I feel less than they?
We were all inmates of one place,
And I, the monarch of each race,
Had power to kill—yet, strange, to tell!
In quiet we had learn'd to dwell—
My very chains and I grew friends,
So much a long communion tends
To make us what we are:—even I
Regain'd my freedom with a sigh.

PART OF THE IIIrd CANTO

OF

CHILDE HAROLD.

Lake Leman woos me with its crystal face,
The mirror where the stars and mountains view
The stillness of their aspect in each trace
Its clear depth yields of their far height and hue:
There is too much of man here, to look through
With a fit mind the might which I behold;
But soon in me shall Loneliness renew
    Thoughts hid, but not less cherish'd than of old,
Ere mingling with the herd had penn'd me in their fold.

Is it not better, then, to be alone,
And love Earth only for its earthly sake?
By the blue rushing of the arrowy Rhone,
Or the pure bosom of its nursing lake,
Which feeds it as a mother who doth make
A fair but froward infant her own care,
Kissing its cries away as these awake; —
    Is it not better thus our lives to wear,
Than join the crushing crowd, doom'd to inflict or bear?

Here the self-torturing sophist, wild Rousseau,
The apostle of affliction, he who threw
Enchantment over passion, and from woe
Wrung overwhelming eloquence, first drew
The breath which made him wretched; yet he knew
How to make madness beautiful, and cast

4*

O'er erring deeds and thoughts, a heavenly hue
Of words, like sunbeams, dazzling as they past
The eyes, which o'er them shed tears feelingly and fast.

His love was passion's essence—as a tree
On fire by lightning; with ethereal flame
Kindled he was, and blasted; for to be
Thus, and enamoured, were in him the same.
But his was not the love of living dame,
Nor of the dead who rise upon our dreams,
But of ideal beauty, which became
In him existence, and o'erflowing teems
Along his burning page, distempered though it seems.

This breathed itself to life in Julie, *this*
Invested her with all that's wild and sweet,
This hallowed, too, the memorable kiss
Which every morn his fevered lip would greet,
From her's, who but with friendship his would meet;
But to that gentle touch, through brain and breast
Flash'd the thrill'd spirit's love-devouring heat;
In that absorbing sigh perchance more blest,
Than vulgar minds may be with all they seek possest.

Clear, placid Leman, thy contrasted lake,
With the wild world I dwelt in, is a thing
Which warns me, with its stillness, to forsake
Earth's troubled waters for a purer spring.
This quiet sail is as a noiseless wing
To waft me from distraction; once I loved
Torn ocean's roar, but thy soft murmuring
Sounds sweet as if a sister's voice reproved,
That I with stern delights should e'er have been so moved.

It is the hush of night, and all between
Thy margin and the mountains, dusk, yet clear,
Mellowed and mingling, yet distinctly seen;
Save darken'd Jura, whose capt heights appear
Precipitously steep; and drawing near,
There breathes a living fragrance from the shore,

Of flowers yet fresh with childhood; on the ear
Drops the light drip of the suspended oar
Or chirps the grasshopper one good-night carol more;

He is an evening reveller, who makes
His life an infancy, and sings his fill;
At intervals, some bird from out the brakes,
Starts into voice a moment, then is still.
There seems a floating whisper on the hill,
But that is fancy, for the starlight dews
All silently their tears of love instil,
Weeping themselves away, till they infuse
Deep into Nature's breast the spirit of her hues.

The sky is changed! — and such a change! Oh night,
And storm, and darkness, ye are wondrous strong,
Yet lovely in your strength, as is the light
Of a dark eye in woman! Far along!
From peak to peak, the rattling crags among
Leaps the live thunder! Not from one lone cloud,
But every mountain now hath found a tongue,
And Jura answers, through her misty shroud
Back to the joyous Alps, who call to her aloud!

And this is in the night : — Most glorious night!
Thou wert not sent for slumber! let me be
A sharer in thy fierce and far delight, —
A portion of the tempest and of thee!
How the lit lake shines, a phosphoric sea,
And the big rain comes dancing to the earth!
And now, again 'tis black, — and now, the glee
Of the loud hills shakes with its mountain mirth,
As if they did rejoice o'er a young earthquake's birth.

Now, where the swift Rhone cleaves his way between
Heights which appear as lovers who have parted
In hate, whose mining depths so intervene,
That they can meet no more, though brokenhearted,
Though in their souls, which thus each other thwarted,
Love was the very root of the fond rage

Which blighted their life's bloom, and then departed : —
Itself expired, but leaving them an age
Of years all winters, — war within themselves to wage.

Now, where the quick Rhone thus hath cleft his way
The mightiest of the storms hath ta'en his stand :
For here not one, but many, make their play,
And fling their thunder-bolts from hand to hand,
Flashing and cast around : of all the band,
The brightest through these parted hills hath fork'd
His lightnings, as if he did understand,
That in such gaps as desolation work'd,
There the hot shaft should blast whatever therein lurk'd.

Sky, mountains, river, winds, lake, lightnings! ye!
With night, and clouds, and thunder, and a soul
To make these felt and feeling, well may be
Things that have made me watchful; the far roll
Of your departing voices, is the knoll
Of what in me is sleepless, — if I rest.
But where of ye, oh tempests! is the goal!
Are ye like those within the human breast,
Or do ye find, at length, like eagles, some high nest!

The morn is up again, the dewy morn,
With breath all incense, and with cheek all bloom,
Laughing the clouds away with playful scorn,
And living as if earth contain'd no tomb, —
And glowing into day : we may resume
The march of our existence : and thus I,
Still on thy shores, fair Leman! may find room
And food for meditation, nor pass by
Much, that may give us pause, if pondered fittingly.

Clarens! sweet Clarens, birth-place of deep Love!
Thine air is the young breath of passionate thought;
Thy trees take root in Love; the snows above
The very Glaciers have his colours caught,
And sun-set into rose-hues sees them wrought
By rays which sleep there lovingly : the rocks,

The permanent crags, tell here of Love, who sought
In them a refuge from the worldly shocks,
Which stir and sting the soul with hope that woos, then mocks.

Clarens! by heavenly feet thy paths are trod,
Undying Love's, who here ascends a throne
To which the steps are mountains; where the god
Is a pervading life and light, — so shown
Not on those summits solely, nor alone
In the still cave and forest; o'er the flower
His eye is sparkling, and his breath hath blown,
His soft and summer breath, whose tender power
Passes the strength of storms in their most desolate hour.

All things are here of *him*; from the black pines,
Which are his shade on high, and the loud roar
Of torrents, where he listeneth, to the vines
Which slope his green path downward to the shore,
Where the bowed waters meet him, and adore,
Kissing his feet with murmurs; and the wood,
The covert of old trees, with trunks all hoar,
But light leaves, young as joy, stands where it stood
Offering to him, and his, a populous solitude.

A populous solitude of bees and birds,
And fairy-form'd and many coloured things,
Who worship him with notes more sweet than words,
And innocently open their glad wings,
Fearless and full of life : the gush of springs,
And fall of lofty fountains, and the bend
Of stirring branches, and the bud which brings
The swiftest thought of beauty, here extend,
Mingling, and made by Love, unto one mighty end.

He who hath loved not, here would learn that lore,
And make his heart a spirit; he who knows
That tender mystery, will love the more,
For this is Love's recess where vain men's woes,
And the world's waste, have driven him far from those,
For 'tis his nature to advance or die;

He stands not still, but or decay's, or grows
Into a boundless blessing, which may vie
With the immortal lights, in its eternity!

'Twas not for fiction chose Rousseau this spot,
Peopling it with affections, but he found
It was the scene which passion must allot
To the mind's purified beings : 'twas the ground
Where early Love his Psyche's zone unbound,
And hallowed it with loveliness, 'tis lone,
And wonderful, and deep, and hath a sound,
And sense, and sight of sweetness; here the Rhone
Hath spread himself a couch, the Alps have rear'd a throne.

Printed in the USA
CPSIA information can be obtained
at www.ICGtesting.com
LVHW010422300923
759528LV00010B/1231